Leading with War

The Fallacies of Team Leadership:

How Leaders Distort and Misuse the Lessons of History

by Martina Sprague

I0470973

Acknowledgements:

Front cover image pictures Napoleon Bonaparte on a horse. Image source: St. James Palace, London, reproduced under Wikimedia Commons license.

Back cover image pictures Sun-tzu, famous Chinese military strategist and author of the *Art of War*. Image source: PD-ART, reproduced under Wikimedia Commons license.

TABLE OF CONTENTS

INTRODUCTION

As evidenced by the immensely large number of leadership books on the market, one tends to think that leadership is a profound subject that needs this much coverage in order that one can make sense of it. "In 1975 two hundred books were published on the subject of managing and leading. By 1997 that number had more than tripled. In fact, over the last twenty years authors have offered up over nine thousand different systems, languages, principles, and paradigms to help explain the mysteries of management and leadership."[1] But many modern ideas about leadership are nothing but hybrids of older ideas, and rarely is an idea truly new. In fact, as American journalist Robert D. Kaplan (1952- CE) observed, "Some truths are so obvious that to mention them in polite company seems either pointless or rude. What is left unstated, however, can with time be forgotten."[2]

Although most of the motivational leadership studies on the market promise to reveal a new and innovative approach to leadership, many cast very little fresh light on the problems the leader faces every day. I believe it is safe to say that many of us read these books not because we seek something concrete that will inform us of how to behave, or that will contradict our previous views and therefore trigger some critical thinking, but because we want confirmation of the views that we already hold. Leading with War, or using examples set by successful military leaders, is but one way that leadership studies are popularly approached. To demonstrate a point, allow me to cherry-pick a sentence or two from the ancient Chinese military classic *The Methods of the Ssu-ma*, dating to approximately the fourth century BCE: "If you lead in person they will follow. When orders are annoying they will be ignored."[3] Or from Sun-tzu's *Art of War*, dating to the fifth to sixth century BCE: "When the troops continually gather in small groups and whisper together, the general has lost the confidence of the army."[4] Who can argue with these words of wisdom? Yet contrary to popular belief, history does NOT repeat itself. Jeffrey Cohn, leadership advisor to chief executives, reminds us that one reason why we are bad at picking good leaders is because, "[a]t best, a 'track record' only tells half of the story. In a new position, the candidate will have to face new obstacles, deal with a new team, manage more people, introduce new products, and do it all without a clear roadmap."[5]

In a perfect world the study of leadership, similarly to the study of history as suggested by Swiss historian Jacob Burckhardt (1818-1897 CE), should not "make us clever for the next time, but make us wise forever."[6] The readers of leadership books would be wise to approach their studies with the same caution as a historian approaches his or her sources of information. You start by asking who wrote the book, what is his or her background, and what are the potential biases hidden within the text. What conviction does the author hold and what is he or she trying to achieve? Historians, as should leaders, deal with what has happened in the past but avoid making predictions or prescribing future behavior. A good historian does not push an ideology. Rather, he or she forms a thesis and examines the issues, and so should the leader. If the evidence reveals that the initial thesis will not work, the historian, as should the leader, changes the thesis rather than cherry-picks for evidence that supports the initial idea. Military historian Jay Luvaas pointed out that, "A book is like a mirror. If an ass looks in, no prophet can peer out."[7] This might be good advice for the leader, too.

The material in this book is excerpted from the previously published book, *Leadership, It Ain't Rocket Science: A Critical Analysis of Moving with the Cheese and Other Motivational Leadership Bullshit*, also by Martina Sprague.

"Experience is of more value in the Art of War than all philosophical truth."

— Carl von Clausewitz

"How fortunate for leaders that men do not think."

— Adolf Hitler

"No man is good enough to govern another man, without that other's consent."

— Abraham Lincoln

THE GREAT GENERALS

Some say that war, however brutal and disgusting we may find it, brings out the finest qualities in leaders: courage, honor, integrity, and, above all, character. The lessons of war serve as popular civilian leadership models. Consider for a moment how leaders on every level of the corporate ladder are likely to identify with the widely quoted *Art of War*, an ancient military text and classic work on strategy by Chinese general and philosopher Sun-tzu (c. 544-496 BCE): "One who knows the enemy and knows himself will not be endangered in a hundred engagements,"[8] or, "Attaining one hundred victories in one hundred battles is not the pinnacle of excellence. Subjugating the enemy's army without fighting is the true pinnacle of excellence."[9] On the home front Robert E. Lee (1807-1870 CE) might be more celebrated than any other American Civil War hero. His character, compassion, and cunning ability to thwart his foes and lead the Confederacy against the Union in what ultimately became a losing battle has been studied, written about, commented upon, and quoted in texts too numerous to mention. Should we study the great generals of history and Lead with War?

Before answering, think about this: To what extent is it true to say that great military leaders are necessarily compassionate with respect to their subordinates or the opposition, or strive to take the ethically high road of winning without fighting? Richard Marcinko (1940- CE) (a.k.a. the Rogue Warrior), former United States Navy SEAL and author of *Leadership Secrets of the Rogue Warrior*, put it simply when he said, "Thou shalt win at all cost,"[10] and, "To survive and succeed, you must accept one plain and painful truth: Business can be war. Life can be war. If you want to win that war: Attack. Attack! ATTACK!"[11] Napoleon Bonaparte (1769-1821 CE), military and political leader during the French Revolution, would have agreed. He saw only one thing—the enemy's main body—and tried to crush it, confident that secondary matters would settle themselves.

As we shall see, leaders and leadership principles are full of contradictions, as reflected in the views of military strategists and generals the world over. For example, as stated by ancient Chinese military strategist Zhuge Liang (181-234 CE), "Military authority, directing the armed forces, is the matter of the authoritative power of the leading general. If the general can hold the authority of the military and operate its power, he oversees his subordinates like a fierce tiger with wings, flying over the four seas, going into action whenever there is an encounter."[12] Contrast his views with United States Army retired Lieutenant General Russel L. Honoré's (1947- CE) opinion that leadership does not simply involve barking orders and expecting results. Even an organization such as the army, where soldiers supposedly are committed to following orders, must remember that people are people first before they are soldiers or subordinates. Even if soldiers have no choice but to follow orders, they still have the power to affect the outcome. The leader should therefore "set people on the right path" rather than boss them, and, according to General Honoré, "do the planning and then to motivate the execution."[13]

A particularly important observation might be General Honoré's view that "[l]eaders should keep dissenters close because they'll provide a valuable perspective."[14] Failing to create a sense of purpose behind the mission will make it difficult to reach efficiency. Unless the team has the proper equipment to execute the plan, no motivation in the world will move them to action. "I was always fond of logistics, even though I was an infantry officer," says Honoré. "So I would drive all my organizations crazy about logistics because logistics was always the hardest thing to get done. So many times units failed, not because they weren't capable but because they didn't get the gas, the boots, and the bullets on time."[15] Can you identify an occasion at your place of employment when you were unable to be as efficient as you would have liked because you could not get the proper equipment to function, or did not have access to the equipment you needed?

Although it is obvious that one can catch more flies with sugar than vinegar, and military personnel as well as employees in the civilian world are less likely to backfire when they believe in the value of the principles they are subjected to, the best way to treat one's subordinates, whether or not to listen to and value their advice and suggestions, appears to be a highly individual matter. As underscored by a former King of Prussia, Frederick the Great (1712-1786 CE), "The general [should] talk of war from time to time with the most enlightened generals of his army . . . and if, in free conversation, they offer good advice, he should profit by it without remarking who has found a good thing; but once it is executed with success, he should say, in the presence of a big group of officers: It is to so-and-so that I owe the success in this affair."[16] Yet on the same subject and in nearly the same era Napoleon said, "In military operations, I consulted no one but myself."[17] American president Abraham Lincoln (1809-1865 CE), who guided America through the devastating experience of the Civil War, supposedly took a different middle of the road type approach: "He met with his generals and cabinet members in their homes, offices, and in the field, principally to provide direction and leadership. He toured the Navy Yard and the fortifications in and around Washington, and inspected new weaponry, all to obtain accurate knowledge of the workings and abilities of the armed forces. This contact also gave him the first-hand knowledge he needed to make informed, accurate decisions without having to rely solely on the word of others."[18] Who was right? Who was the better leader?

What we can learn from these examples is that there are different perspectives on leadership that we tend to cherry-pick as we see fit. Yes, we admire Robert E. Lee because he had character and led from the front with purpose and direction, motivating and instilling pride in those he led, as relayed in this account by H. W. Crocker III:

> If Lee respected the rights of his superiors, he also respected his subordinates. For one thing, he treated them as adults. His method of leadership was far removed from the childish ersatz challenges and rewards contemporary managers like to dangle

before their employees—selecting managers-of-the-month, gathering self-conscious "team" cheerleading sessions, organizing weekend whitewater rafting or mountain climbing to teach "leadership" and "teamwork". . . A business should be what the Army of Northern Virginia was: a "voluntary association of gentlemen organized for the sole purpose" of one's enterprise. That purpose is best achieved, and one's subordinates are best inspired, by doing, not by playing games and offering carnival prizes.[19]

But while we admire Robert E. Lee for his character, we simultaneously admire Napoleon, not because of his character, but because he knew how to win. Winning matters perhaps even more than how one plays the game. To retain leadership a leader must succeed more often than he loses. But shalt thou really win at all cost, as stressed by the Rogue Warrior Richard Marcinko? Is business really war? In addition to requiring an enormous personal sacrifice from each member of his team, the Rogue Warrior might be too tough to stomach for most people. Not only does he agree with Friedrich Nietzsche's (1844-1900 CE) dictum, "Whatever does not break my back makes me stronger," but thinks that a manager should demand that his subordinates work so hard that it literally hurts. However, this is often not possible because in our "soft" world, as Marcinko suggests, such a manager would be "branded as a tyrant or sadist."[20]

So who is right: Robert E. Lee or Richard Marcinko? When attempting to answer this question, one might start by asking whether it is true that what does not break your back makes you stronger. The problem with making assumptions, says the Rogue Warrior, is that "when people assume things, they generally think that everyone else . . . is making the same assumptions."[21] Yet, he does just this—assume—when quoting Nietzsche's dictum. Few people would be willing to sacrifice their health, sleep, well-being, or family for their boss or company, even if the pain is more mental than physical in the civilian world of business. Are these people necessarily lazy and poor team players?

Although he has no doubt offered much insight into successful leadership strategies; for example, that one's vision must be "sensible, achievable, and personally rewarding" to inspire the employees to achieve it,[22] the Rogue Warrior's principles are full of contradictions not just when compared with those of civilian leaders, but when compared with statements made by other important military figures. For example, George Patton (1885-1945 CE), who the Rogue Warrior quoted, is perhaps best known for his leadership skills in commanding armies in World War II: "The time to take counsel of your fears is before you make an important battle decision . . . Any man who is afraid to die will never really live!"[23] But before you take this statement to heart, consider for a moment the views of the much celebrated United States Air Force test pilot Chuck Yeager (1923- CE), who broke the sound barrier in 1947: "I was always afraid of dying. Always. It was my fear that made me learn everything I could about my airplane and my emergency equipment, and kept me flying respectful of my machine and always alert in the cockpit. If you want to grow old as a pilot, you've got to know when to push it, and when to back off."[24]

Chuck Yeager was so afraid of dying that he could not afford to make mistakes. His views communicate the value attached to understanding one's capabilities and limitations. Richard Hiner, retired as vice president of training from the AOPA (Aircraft Owners and Pilots Association and Air Safety Foundation), stated in a newsletter in 2005:

> During a flight review, a well-seasoned pilot posed a question that I had never before been asked. "After all your hours in the air, do you still get butterflies in your stomach when you climb into the cockpit?" "Yes," I responded, "and if they ever go away, I'll stop flying." This pilot thought that a little fear and anxiety was a sign of weakness or a lack of skill, something to be avoided. Au contraire, I told him; it keeps you sharp, gives you an edge, and causes you to check and recheck the airplane, the weather, and your own physical and mental condition before taking to the air. A little fear and anxiety is something to be encouraged, not resisted.[25]

What should be learned from these examples

is that it is healthy to ask what can be achieved at your particular place on the leadership ladder. As Norse historian Snorri Sturluson (1178-1241 CE) reminded us nearly a millennium ago, "Consider with thyself what thou art man enough to undertake . . . for to take up great resolutions, and then to lay them aside, would only end in dishonor."[26] Thus when the price becomes greater than the value, it is prudent to cut your losses and run. In his book, *A First-Rate Madness: Uncovering the Links Between Leadership and Mental Illness*, Nassir Ghaemi reminds us that "an excess of virtue is a vice," and advises us to "recall that the classical Greek concept of virtue, derived from Aristotle, involved moderation":

> Too much virtue converts courage to recklessness, for instance. It may be legitimate to turn around and flee, rather than fight, under the right circumstances. That is what Aristotle meant by virtue, not some ideal of never-changing steadfastness. Given this perspective, one cannot cleanly separate virtue from vice, for the virtue of courage sometimes involves fighting, sometimes retreating, sometimes charging—each action interpretable as vices of violence, cowardice, and recklessness.[27]

Leadership is not war, nor is business war as claimed by the Rogue Warrior. Leadership and business are not wars any more than the war on drugs or the war on illiteracy are wars. *Thou shalt not win at all cost, lest thou might score a pyrrhic victory when the opposition rises up to smite thee.* There is more to success than Attack. Attack! ATTACK! The Rogue Warrior's "missions were deadly and difficult," which placed him in position to "expect nothing less from [his] men than total dedication and absolute competence."[28] But if you want to use the underlying principles of attack in non-deadly business endeavors, you cannot take them literally. Although leadership is about character (or to extend the cliché: Leadership is to *have* character but not *be* a character), it is NOT about flattering yourself over your ability to think up clever slogans. And even character cannot win if the strategy is poor, as demonstrated in the following example:

> The impeachment of [President] Bill Clinton over his affair with Monica Lewinsky, a White House intern, brought forth years of pontification on sex and politics. The implication was, for Clinton critics, that a good president had to display "good character"—kindness, moral rectitude, self-control, and so on. "Character above all" became the mantra (the title, for instance, of a PBS broadcast subtitled "An Exploration of Presidential Leadership." [Yet] journalist Ronald Kessler titled his sympathetic biography of [President George W.] Bush "A Matter of Character," and emphasized how Bush's superior behavior made him a

better leader than Clinton. Bush had more sexual continence than Clinton; he may have been better behaved with staff; he may have been more normal and decent. But all that might argue against, not for, better leadership skills as a president in time of crisis.[29]

Which view you take may be a matter of your political stand. However, to make the best use of the insights the great historical generals offer us (and of the insights offered by journalists and lay people as well), we must watch for source bias, place their views in proper perspective, and understand that the information must be modified to be used successfully within our own particular organization. Let us look at a few historical accounts of warfare from the perspectives of the generals and the soldiers. As you read these brief summaries, consider whether or not you would have liked to serve in these wars under these leaders. What makes you tick and what doesn't, and why? If you desire to Lead with War, I would recommend reading these accounts in their entirety as a basic education in different leadership styles. Most of them are available for free online.

THUCYDIDES (c. 460-395 BCE)

Thucydides, a Greek historian and Athenian general, credited with writing the *History of the Peloponnesian War* between the Athens Empire and the Peloponnesian League led by Sparta in the fifth century BCE, believed that the twenty-seven year long conflict (431-404 BCE) with a six-year interlude of peace, which ended with Athens' surrender to Sparta, was one of the greatest wars that had taken place among the Greek, a belief he based on the examination of earlier wars: ". . . looking into times of past, I have yet light on to persuade me, I do not think they have been very great, either for matter of war or otherwise."[30]

Thucydides wrote from the perspective of a man directly involved in the war as opposed to reflecting on it after it had ended. But he was not an eye-witness to every event. So when interpreting the account, the historian must be aware of possible biases. Simultaneously Thucydides had a unique way of weighing one side of the conflict against the other and demonstrated little hope of winning the war for Athens. Since the conflict was one of the greatest that had taken place among the Greek, he found it crucial to relate it to future generations. His writings provide good insight into human nature and the difficulties of judging war objectively: "And though men always judge the present war wherein they live to be greatest, and when it is past, admire more those that were before it, yet if they consider of this war by the acts done in the same, it will manifest itself to be greater than any of those before mentioned."[31]

The uncertainty of life in Greece and the many enemy invasions created reluctance among the citizens to settle permanently and work the fields, and many left for Athens, the most potent and stable of all cities, which grew large as a result. Thucydides spends considerable time exploring Greek life and laying the foundation for the conflict. For example, he notes how houses were unfenced and traveling unsafe because thieves were crossing from one island to another. The people had to accustom themselves to wearing armor and building walls around their cities. He makes references to the taking of Troy, which demonstrates that he knew his history, and further educates the reader about the wealth of Greece, the wars fought between Athens and Aegina, one of the Greek islands, and the great power of the Greek navies that exercised dominion over other peoples.

Sparta, however, became a powerful enemy of Athens despite the fact that it was sparsely decorated and constructed with scattered villages and, thus, to an observer would seem the least powerful of the two and definitely inferior to Athens. The Athenians and the Spartans divided themselves into leagues, the Athenians with command of the sea and the Spartans with command of the land. The dangers experienced in the long lasting war sharpened the military edge of both Athens and Sparta. Yet Thucydides admits that it was difficult to know the certainty of what took place, because many people had spoken of many things. For example, of the long speeches of the assembly between the Corinthians and the Corcyraeans which are related in the *History of the Peloponnesian War*, one speech covers a full seven pages and is unlikely accurate word for word, although it may well be accurate in overall content.

On several occasions Thucydides demonstrates how victory is subjective: First the Corinthians set up a trophy. Then the Corcyraeans, "as if they had the victory, set up a trophy likewise."[32] The Corinthians believed they were victorious, because they had caused more destruction and killed more of the enemy. The Corcyraeans believed they were victorious, because they had sunk thirty galleys of the Corinthians and recovered many dead bodies, and also because the Corinthians had the previous day rowed away from them, which could be viewed either as an act of cowardice or defeat. Thucydides also provides good insight into how Sparta justified the war against Athens, which is particularly interesting because of his position as an Athenian general. For example, he relates how Sthenelaidas stood up and spoke to the Lacedaemonians (Spartans) about the actions of the Athenians:

> For though they have been much in their own praises, yet they have said nothing to the contrary but that they have done injury to our confederates . . . Let no man tell me that after we have once received injury we ought to deliberate. No, it belongs rather to the doers of injury to spend time in consultation. Wherefore, men of Lacedaemon, decree the war, as becometh the dignity of Sparta; and let not the Athenians grow yet greater, nor let us betray our confederates, but in the name of the Gods proceed against

the doers of injustice.[33]

Additionally, the Lacedaemonians, the ambassadors of the several confederates, and the Corinthians spoke to the effect:

> For though it be the part of discreet men to be quiet unless they have wrong, yet it is the part of valiant men, when they receive injury, to pass from peace into war, and after success, from war to come again to composition, and neither to swell with the good success of war not to suffer injury through pleasure taken in the ease of peace.[34]

History supposedly informs the actions of the future leadership. Yet Thucydides acknowledged that leadership cannot be based on historical events, and that leaders tend to distort the truth to benefit their particular aim. He believed that there are essentially three elements responsible for war: honor, fear, and interest. Going to war is honorable in the sense that a man fights for his state and its citizen, which allows him to build a reputation that distinguishes him from the masses; fear causes people to form into groups for common protection against enemies; and interest results from wanting something for personal gain. The challenges of war are many: "Consider before you enter how unexpected the chances of war be. For a long war for the most part endeth in calamity . . . And men, when they go to war, use many times to fall first to action . . . and when they have taken harm, then they fall to reasoning."[35] How often do you see in your own organization new ideas implemented with great enthusiasm but little forethought, and first when the leaders "have taken harm" do they "fall to reasoning"? Thucydides might have had an aversion to conflict, or he might just have been an insightful man. He also warns us: "For no man comes to execute a thing with the same confidence he premeditates it. For we deliver opinions in safety, whereas in the action itself we fail through fear."[36]

Although he understood the calamity brought by war, Thucydides simultaneously believed that if one is to retain power for future generations, then enemies must be resisted in any and every way. The natural law of humanity is that the weaker are subject to the stronger, and those who are stronger can naturally use their strength to force their subjects into compliance. Thus the strong do what they can and the weak suffer what they must. Tyrants, who are often the heads of states or the leaders in war, tend to provide only for themselves, their own comfort, and the aggrandizement of their immediate family. Needless to say, this sort of self-aggrandizement among the leadership creates injustices and tends to sabotage the subordinates' willingness to follow. In a civilian business where the subordinates generally have more say than in the army, a tyrant leader would have difficulty bringing his team to action.

Thucydides further observes that when the leadership is just, a great tower of strength can be created even when the populace must sacrifice. Kindness, when shown at the proper time, has great power to remove grievances that would otherwise stand in one's way and sabotage the team's motivation to pursue the goal. From Athenian statesman Pericles' (c. 495-429 BCE) funeral oration delivered at the end of the first year of the Peloponnesian War, we can deduce that it is crucial that ordinary citizens occupy themselves with the affairs of the state:

> Our public men have, besides politics, their private affairs to attend to, and our ordinary citizens, though occupied with the pursuits of industry, are still fair judges of public matters; for, unlike any other nation, regarding him who takes no part in these duties not as unambitious but as useless, we Athenians are able to judge at all events if we cannot originate, and instead of looking on discussion as a stumbling-block in the way of action, we think it an indispensable preliminary to any wise action at all.[37]

How can the ideas in this speech be applied to leadership in today's civilian workplace? If the employees take no interest in the affairs of the company for which they work, they become useless (or nearly so) to the company. And, as Pericles notes, debate and discussion should not be viewed as a stumbling-block in the way of action, but as a crucial necessity to wise action.

Furthermore, the Athenians compared themselves to their rivals, the Spartans, who in essence took their young from the cradle and, using iron discipline, educated them in matters of war. The Athenians, by contrast, would live exactly as they pleased, and yet were "just as ready to encounter every legitimate danger."[38] So how do we know just how much discipline the leadership should exercise on their subordinates to remain effective in reaching their goals? In Sparta every man was a soldier and owed strict obedience to the state, while in Athens life was more lenient. Yet both Sparta and Athens were great states that had the potential for great accomplishments.

The strength of Thucydides' account lies in his observations of human nature, and many of his ideas, although nearly two thousand five hundred years old, could as well have been written today. Not much has changed. Few are those who view current events with a critical eye, he notes. Rather than questioning and investigating various claims of "truth," we tend to readily accept whatever story is handed us through tradition. Consider in your own organization the leadership's fondness of popular sayings intended to inspire the employees. Yet neither the leadership nor the employees typically spend more than the briefest of moments (if that) to question the validity of such slogans as, "You manage things but lead people." These slogans are used not necessarily because they speak the truth, but because they are attractive at truth's expense.

Thucydides also stresses inexperience or lack of insight as the common factors that make people eager to take up arms. In civilian leadership, are we not more prone to go along with new ideas that we have not fully discussed or thought about while we are still young and inexperienced? As we get older, we know more, think more, rely more on past experiences, and therefore frequently become more resistant to change. Many of Thucydides' insights thus seem well suited for modern inspirational books about leadership. But to use them in earnest, they must be examined in deeper context. If we "admire more those [wars] that were before," do we really have a clear perspective on the conflicts of our own time? And, if not, how can we use historical wisdom to gain that perspective?

XENOPHON (c. 431-354 BCE)

The March Up Country is the report of Xenophon's return from Persia where he has been aiding Cyrus the Younger in an attempt to take the throne from Cyrus' own brother, Artaxerxes II. In this detailed and with few exceptions trustworthy account of the Greek mercenaries' long march back to the sea, Xenophon, the protagonist of the story, an Athenian soldier and a pupil and admirer of Socrates, is elected to a leadership position after the death of Cyrus the Younger. Serving alongside of Cheirisophos, the commanding officer, he leads the Greek mercenaries, known as the Ten Thousand, through hostile territory to the Black Sea. Written objectively in clear prose that lacks splendor and exaggeration, the account describes the rigors, difficult terrain and weather, and the troops' encounters with enemy forces. The account is considered a classical historical work. Perhaps what makes it particularly unique is that the events the mercenaries encounter during the march portray no major battles but picture the army in defeat.

Since the army is constantly challenged by the enemy, Xenophon has several opportunities to act on his leadership skills. The first noteworthy mention is his professionalism in the form of strong and fair leadership. Always ready to listen to his troops, he is a passionate but realistic leader who employs an open-door policy where "anyone might come to him, at breakfast or supper, or if he slept could awake him, and tell anything he had to propose for the war."[39] Although self-critical in the analysis of his skills, he portrays himself as a slightly more just leader than Cheirisophos, who lashes out and strikes a guide in anger; an act of violence, which Xenophon describes as carelessness and perhaps the fundamental difference between himself and Cheirisophos. How Xenophon handles the difficulties related to motivating the tired, hungry, and cold troops is another testament to his compassion and ability as a leader. He starts by begging the weary troops not to stay behind as the enemy is on the chase. But when the men, too tired to move, ask that he cut their throats instead and go on without them, for "march they could not," he succumbs to their wishes to settle down for the night, "without fire or food, after posting such guards as he could."[40]

Each segment of the march, broken into measurements of stages and leagues, provides vivid images of the terrain and weather. When the troops get over the height where Tiribazos, the lieutenant-governor of Southern Armenia, means to attack them, they march "three desert stages, 15 leagues," and reach the River Euphrates which they cross "waist-deep," then move on through deep snow with a north wind blowing in their faces.[41] Xenophon's insightful details of the hardships they encounter can be described only by someone who has been there and done that. The insulating powers of the snow, for example, "kept them snug and warm where they lay unless it slipt off."[42] Good advice to help the poor state of the troops is given without exaggeration: The blinding effect of the snow is countered by holding "something black before their eyes," and frostbite is handled by taking their shoes off at night, for the newly flayed raw leather straps from untanned hides would otherwise work its way into their feet when the shoes froze.[43]

Xenophon's thoughtful strategic battle considerations add realism and credibility to the account. Prisoners are taken alive to act as guides, and language barriers are bridged with the help of interpreters. Great attention to detail is employed when describing the problems of defense during river crossings: "They could not go through the river in arms, or else the river carried them off; they could not carry the arms on their heads, or they were bare against arrows and other missiles."[44] The enemy is portrayed in simple and objective terms as "very good bowmen" with considerable skill at constructing strong weapons that could penetrate both shield and corselet. War casualties are acknowledged and the dead given "all the honours customary for brave men, as far as possible."[45]

When the morale of the Hellenes dwindles, leaving them without hope, Xenophon looks for alternate and more suitable routes to help men and animals pass with greater ease, or as an option, place the troops above the enemy on higher and more favorable ground. He offers ready answers to Cheirisophos' problems by suggesting that they not fight the enemy in lines but in company columns, which attests to his concern for the morale and safety of the men. A line will break at once due to the difficulty of the mountain terrain, he reasons, and such a break would demoralize the men and endanger the whole group. Instead, he suggests, the columns can come to the aid of one another and create difficulties for an enemy attempting to penetrate the spaces between them. The strongest should go on first, and the columns should be placed so far apart that the "extreme columns overlap the enemy wings."[46] A great deal of thought has obviously been afforded the issue of teamwork.

However, the detailed and matter-of-fact style of the writing lacks emotion and greater drama, and very little is told about the individual persons making up the Ten Thousand. In fact, the greatest dramatic moment may come when they finally observe the sea at Trebizond. The account as a whole is particularly interesting considering the fact that it portrays the actions taken after defeat rather than victory. The reactions of the men to the sight of the Black Sea, and the welcoming provisions of their countrymen in the Hellenic city of Euxine in the Colchian country, may be viewed as a victory in itself. Xenophon's memory of some of the details of the story can be questioned, considering that he wrote it sometime after his exile from Athens. His use of dream interpretation to determine the course of action seems a bit contrary to his otherwise brilliant leadership skills. But the reliance on dreams in story telling frequently comes in handy in ancient literature when few other options remain.

When studying *The March Up Country*, one might keep in mind that Xenophon was not just another soldier; he was in a leadership position and elected to this role when the Ten Thousand Greek were without a leader in hostile territory. Might his leadership role have influenced his desire for victory or how he portrayed the difficulties they encountered including the morale of the men? Might it have forced him to analyze events and think of solutions? Or might it have made him trivialize the difficulties so that the men would appear stronger than they were to convey a more positive account for future generations? Despite the fact that some historians like to place this ancient narrative in the "Great Man" category (implying that successes are largely determined by a single human being—a great man—and not by political or environmental circumstances), my view is that the text as a whole seems honest, avoids exaggeration, and examines the boundaries of human capability. As an autobiographical account written from a third person perspective, it is largely void of personal opinion or emotion.

JULIUS CAESAR (c. 100-44 BCE)

Julius Caesar was a Roman statesman and military leader with ambitions to conquer Gaul to extend his dominions and neutralize any threats against his empire. His reputation as a strong military leader and strategist is clearly demonstrated in *De Bello Gallico & Other Commentaries of Caius Julius Caesar*, and it is not for nothing that he took the title of dictator (one who gives orders). The story is recounted from the position of a man who is clearly offense/attack oriented and finds it "better to be slain in battle than not to recover [our] ancient glory in war."[47] At times he is bold to the point of being reckless. The *Commentaries* start by giving the reasons for the unrest: Gaul was entering into a confederacy against the Roman people because they feared that the Roman army would be led against them. The fact that the Roman army passed the winter in Gaul caused a great deal of concern among the Gallic people and some were anxious for a revolution.

The *Commentaries* are easy to read, full of graphic description, and rich in detail regarding battle strategies, architectures of forts and walls, and descriptions of battlegrounds. For example, "A hill, declining evenly from the top, extended to the river Sambre," which depth was about three feet, and a second hill "of like ascent . . . and open from about 200 paces at the lowest part; but in the upper part, woody . . . [made it] not easy to see through it."[48] When organizing for battle, the standard is displayed signaling the necessity to run to arms, with signal also given by trumpet to call the soldiers back who had left to seek materials for the rampart. When the battle order is formed, the soldiers are encouraged and watchword given. The battle organization described in the account reinforces the idea that the soldiers were largely self-reliant and able to teamwork to take advantage of opportunities as they arose. "[H]aving been trained by former engagements," the soldiers could suggest to themselves what to do, making it possible to proceed without a leader present at every moment: "[O]n account of the near approach and the speed of the enemy, [they] did not then wait for any command from Caesar."[49] The strategy consists of dividing the forces of the enemy, "so that it might not be necessary to engage with so large a number at one time."[50]

Caesar inquires of the hostages and captives to collect information about the enemy. Information is also carried to him through scouts and letters. He portrays a rather negative image of enemy discipline, as he observes the enemy "marching out of their camp at the second watch, with great noise and confusion, in no fixed order, nor under any command, since each sought for himself the foremost place in the journey, and hastened to reach home, they made their departure appear very like a flight."[51] The cavalry of the Treviri, a tribe of the Gauls, whose reputation for courage is extraordinary, is much alarmed, but when they see the Roman camp filled with enemy forces, hard pressed, they hasten home to relate that the Romans have been conquered.

Caesar also balances this negative account by describing the enemy as having such great courage that "when the foremost of them had fallen, the next stood upon them . . . and fought from their bodies," and those who survived "cast their weapons against our men, as from a mound [of dead bodies]."[52] Simultaneously he portrays himself in a good light and praises his soldiers. For example, when addressing the legions, he does so one by one. When he says he "would raise the siege, if they felt the scarcity too severely, they unanimously begged him not to do so; that they had served for several years under his command in such manner, that they never submitted to insult, and never abandoned an enterprise without accomplishing it; that they should consider it a disgrace if they abandoned the siege after commencing it."[53] One wonders if these are really the words of the legions, or Caesar's own words trying to paint a picture of greater support than he had.

Critognatus, a Gallic noble holds an interesting speech about the disgracefulness of surrender, even as supplies are running short: "To be unable to bear privation for a short time is disgraceful cowardice, not true valour. Those who voluntarily offer themselves to death are more easily found than those who would calmly endure distress . . . What courage do you think would our relatives and friends have, if eighty thousand men were butchered in one spot."[54] Did Caesar learn a valuable lesson in leadership from pondering his enemy's speech when he said that "[i]t is easier to find men who will volunteer to die, than to find those who are willing to endure pain with patience"?

In regards to counting war casualties, it would have been interesting to know how many men Caesar lost. He describes the enemy losses as quite severe. When the enemy surrenders and sends ambassadors to Caesar, and recounts the calamity of their state, "their senators were reduced from 600 to three; that from 60,000 men they were reduced to scarcely 500 who could bear arms"[55]

Overall, Caesar comes across as a rather unpleasant personality to friend and foe alike. He shows little compassion for the troops. For example, he "censure[s] the rashness and avarice of his soldiers" and accuses them of being arrogant, "because they thought that they knew more than their general concerning victory, and the issue of actions: and that he required in his soldiers forbearance and self-command, not less than valour and magnanimity."[56] His harshness is in stark contrasts to the accounts of Thucydides and Xenophon. Despite his unpleasant appearance, however, Caesar does take the time to recognize his lieutenants by naming them. For example, Quintus Pedius, Lucius Aurunculeius Cotta, and Titus Labienus are mentioned in the text.[57] He motivates the troops by proposing "a reward for those who should first scale the walls."[58] I question, however, whether Caesar really was as observant to non-military detail as is described. His account of how "the matrons begin to cast their clothes and silver over the wall, and bending over as far as the lower part of their bosom, with outstretched hands,"[59] certainly gives a vivid image that entertains the reader, but to what extent is it true?

JOHANN VON EWALD (1744-1813 CE)

Let us jump forward a couple of thousand years to near modern day. The diary of Johann von Ewald, a Hessian infantry officer from the Germanic regiments who fought for the English in the American Revolutionary War, is a touching eye-opener for those desiring to experience the American triumph as seen from the viewpoint of the opposition. The diary, covering the period between 1776 and 1784, appears to have been written systematically at the end of each day, until Ewald fell ill and missed recording several months of events. The day-by-day writings are delivered in short segments recording the happenings of morning, afternoon, and evening, and as such present an easy to read first-person view of the war translated into modern English.

The basic and rather non-analytic recounts of events display little emotion initially and, although many details are expressed, fail to give the reader a good visual image of the happenings. For example, Ewald records that his regiment took several casualties, but says nothing about how these men died or how their deaths affected the morale of the troops. When losing a very good friend, he simply states that he regretted the loss. Occasionally, when Ewald observes the enemy, the descriptions become more vivid: "[W]e ran into two riflemen at a bend in the road who, because of the hard rain and wind behind us, had their faces so hidden under their round hats that they were not aware of us."[60] This seems to indicate that Ewald preferred to articulate the observations he made of the enemy rather than embark on a more introspective journey of his own regiment.

The men in Ewald's regiment were mainly recruited in Germany and hired out by the German leaders. Because of their status as foreign conscripts fighting for the English, the Hessian soldiers probably did not earn a significant salary. One might wonder how motivated they were to pursue the war. It seems reasonable, as Ewald states, that they "wanted to spare the King's subjects and hoped to terminate the war amicably,"[61] but he also seems frustrated with the delay of the English: "I see, they do not want to finish the war!"[62] His comment reinforces the belief that motivation to fight was rather slim for the Hessian soldiers. On several occasions Ewald displays empathy for the enemy, for example, when trying to convince the people of the plantation where he is staying that there is, in fact, humane persons in the Hessian army: To "invite their good will and gratitude" he "gave them every protection."[63] However, he also shows signs of arrogance when laughing in the face of the town councilor of Burlington, perhaps as a result of his recent successful patrol, attributed to stormy weather, which precluded the enemy parties from crossing the road. He seems to find pleasure in the opportunity to identify himself as a Hessian soldier to the tenants of a house, telling them they are his prisoners: "The ladies fell at my knees and begged me to leave them their husbands."[64]

The diary becomes particularly absorbing when Ewald receives the message of George Washington's surprise attack on the regiments on the day after Christmas, and "a second messenger of doom arrived, confirming the report and adding that all had been taken prisoner."[65] Ewald's opinion that "the fate of entire kingdoms often depend upon a few blockheads of irresolute men," presents an interesting revelation about the English leadership.[66] He is clearly disgusted with how the English army has been "put to such poor use that eight campaigns were lost" and "thirteen provinces" which has "torn down the Crown of England from its loftiest peak."[67] A wonderful analogy is made when Ewald realizes the reversal of his fate: Four weeks ago, the English had expected to win the war and now "had to render Washington the honor of thinking about our defense." Since the English army had so underestimated their enemy, such fright came over the men that "from this unhappy day onward we saw everything through a magnifying glass."[68]

A curious shift in the way the events are recorded takes place in the supplement to the diary, after the peace is concluded and the United States has been declared independent. Now that the war is over, the diary becomes more introspective and, as a result, the reader can easily identify both with the Americans and Ewald, and with that idea of "Liberty and Independence" for which the Americans were willing to "have their arms and legs smashed."[69] Ewald starts by recounting the losses of the war and, while waiting his turn to ship back home, takes the opportunity to journey to West Point. It becomes obvious that he harbors certain awe for the badly supplied American forces that stubbornly refused to give in to the English. The comparison made between the American army "in its wretched condition," and the "splendid and formidable army of the English"[70] during

Ewald's visit to West Point is especially revealing. The men on the parade ground "looked haggard and pallid and were poorly dressed. Indeed, very many stood quite proudly under arms without shoes and stockings,"[71] and officers who had "marched without shoes . . . still did everything that was possible to live in this world as free men."[72]

When the time comes for Ewald to board the ship and leave for Europe, he displays real longing for the "new country," where on all corners the flag of thirteen stripes is flying and the shores are crowded with people throwing their hats in the air and screaming with joy. The final blow comes when Ewald returns home and fails to receive recognition for the eight years he has spent abroad fighting a war that, in his opinion, was unwinnable. All "services performed were forgotten" and the Hessian soldiers were forced to bend their "proud backs under everything, because it could not be otherwise."[73]

Overall, the insights displayed in Johann von Ewald's diary are deep and appear truthful. For example, when one has nothing left to lose and nothing more to gain, one does what one must do. Ewald believed that Washington, despite the wretched condition of his troops, "would still undertake something, especially when he was in a position to lose everything otherwise."[74] The diary—displaying two continents, two peoples, but separated perhaps by more than the distance of an ocean—certainly gives the reader the opportunity to experience the spirit of the military practices of the time. After the end of the war, many Hessian soldiers remained in America. A large number had also died during the war, either in action or from disease.

Ewald recorded the losses of the Hessian Corps alone in numbers nearing 6,000. The diary is a good book for those Americans who wish to experience their triumph as seen through the eyes of the opposition.

ARMAND DE CAULAINCOURT (1773-1827 CE)

Before his fall from power, and despite what in some people's eyes was a laughable physical stature of merely five feet two inches, Napoleon Bonaparte managed to reach astounding successes in his military campaigns and was thereby able to rise to magnificent heights as ruler of large parts of Western Europe. Although Napoleon is said to have been able to inspire others because he had such a fine sense of the impact that morale had on warfare, not all who served under him agreed. The memoirs by Armand de Caulaincourt, who served under Napoleon during his disastrous campaign into Russia in 1812, read like a novel and discuss Caulaincourt's relationship with the Emperor in a way that indicates that he had intimate knowledge of Napoleon's thoughts. Napoleon relied on Caulaincourt's opinions of how to proceed; although, according to Caulaincourt, "the Emperor delivered a rapid fire of questions and of the answers that he wished to hear," as a result of his hunger for battle.[75] Napoleon also proved gloomy when he feared that the Russian army might escape him, and that he might not, "for some time, obtain the battle he desired so keenly."[76]

Entering the army at fifteen years of age, Armand de Caulaincourt served for a long time without achieving any significant rank. Eventually he rose in rank and went to St. Petersburg on Napoleon's insistence, where he was officially an ambassador but probably more likely a spy; although, spies were said to have been "useless from the moment we crossed on to Russian soil,"[77] which was also why prisoners who could supply information proved crucial. In fact, Napoleon considered the war inconclusive unless prisoners were taken, and "[s]everal times he asked, of the officers who came with reports of our successes, where the prisoners were who ought to have been captured."[78]

Napoleon went to Russia to "finish off, once and for all, the Colossus of Northern Barbarism," so that it would not "interfere with civilized Europe."[79] One might question, however, whether it really was his fear of barbarism and not the hunger for a campaign that made him go. Or as Caulaincourt states, "The Emperor was so anxious for a battle that he drove the army forward with all his energy."[80] Appearing to have wanted the war regardless of any advice he received to the contrary, Napoleon was beaming with pride at the opportunity to measure "his strength with the enemy and obtaining a result that should give some colour to his expedition."[81]

Napoleon's hunger for battle is emphasized throughout the text, and Caulaincourt seems almost fearful at times when he knows the Emperor is being foolhardy. He describes Napoleon as bad tempered. When he accidentally falls of his horse, "his bad temper and forebodings were obvious despite his efforts at concealment," and he "did all he could to dispel the misgivings which he sensed that everyone must have felt—for men are superstitious despite themselves."[82] When one of his men jumped into the water to save another man, Napoleon felt that such a deed was praiseworthy only in civilian life, but not appropriate "to a colonel at the head of his regiment in the face of the enemy."[83] This is indeed an interesting viewpoint. Although avoiding distractions and remaining at your position in time of war is no doubt important, failing to save a team member would likely weaken rather than strengthen unit cohesion and trust.

Caulaincourt further portrays Napoleon as selfish, driven, lacking compassion, and incompetent due to his refusal to accept the advice given him, even as the men were unable to go on because of the lack of supplies. When informed that men and horses had reached the end of their rope, that the marches were too long and exhausting, the "Emperor paid no attention."[84] According to Caulaincourt, the Emperor was ready to pay any price to reach his objective, and the miserable troops almost wished their horses would die, for it would mean the breakdown of their service and "thus the end to their personal privations," which Caulaincourt considered "the secret and cause of our earlier disasters and of our final reverse."[85] But since the Emperor was unwilling to hear the truth, it had no effect on him. In fact, he was "aggravated with those who had the courage to tell it."[86]

Although Napoleon is portrayed in an exceedingly negative light, one might question whether Caulaincourt displays this image of the Emperor because Caulaincourt was opposed to the war and had asked to be excused from it. Yet the idea that peace was "forever represented by the Emperor as the motive of all his enterprises,"[87] reinforces the notion that a leader can justify his obsession with a goal as long as he can convince his team that it rests on a sound foundation (in this case, peace). Is there a risk that a passionate leader might lead his team down the wrong trench?

THE ALLURING FORMULA OF WAR

As demonstrated through the previous examples, one can no doubt be enlightened by viewing leadership through a military prism. War is a profoundly human experience and as such is guided by human emotions and passion. But would those who have fought on our battlefields really recommend war as a classroom for learning team leadership in the civilian workplace? Do civilian businessmen and women and military personnel really understand each other? What problems might one face as a result of a desire to Lead with War?

Although it is tempting to draw parallels between combat leadership and civilian leadership, the lessons of war are unpredictable and cannot be formed into a list of prescribed solutions to particular problems. According to a handbook about *Infantry in Battle* based on studies of World War experiences, and first prepared under the direction of Colonel George C. Marshall (1880-1959 CE):

> The art of war has no traffic with rules, for the infinitely varied circumstances and conditions of combat never produce exactly the same situation twice . . . It follows, then, that the leader who would become a competent tactician must first close his mind to the alluring formula that well-meaning people offer in the name of victory. To master his difficult art he must learn to cut to the heart of a situation,

recognize its decisive elements and base his course of action on these. The ability to do this is not God-given, nor can it be acquired overnight; it is a process of years. He must realize that training in solving problems of all types, long practice in making clear, unequivocal decisions, the habit of concentrating on the question at hand, and an elasticity of mind, are indispensable requisites for the successful practice of the art of war. The leader who frantically strives to remember what someone else did in some slightly similar situation has already set his feet on a well-traveled road to ruin.[88]

The previous paragraph offers food for thought for the aspiring and field-tested leader alike: Leadership is comprised of "infinitely varied circumstances" . . . it "never produce[s] exactly the same situation twice" . . . one must "close [one's] mind to the alluring formula that well-meaning people offer" . . . leadership is "not God-given" and cannot "be acquired overnight; it is a process of years." (Are leaders born or made?) What does this tell us? It suggests that those pursuing leadership in earnest might be wise to avoid trampling the path prescribed by well-meaning but gung-ho men and women who spend their days dreaming up all sorts of bumper sticker slogans which, although possibly proving motivational for a day, lack substance in the real world.

Carl von Clausewitz (1780-1831 CE), an early nineteenth century Prussian soldier and military theorist, concluded that although victory in combat lies in the planning, determining truth or falsehood at any particular moment often proves to be a gamble and chance, an inherent element of war, tends to sabotage the best-laid plans.[89] A talented leader can hope for a strong position in the world only when his character and familiarity with leadership fortify each other, and only when he obeys his own principles which result from his own judgment. But he cannot necessarily expect a subordinate to embrace those same principles, unless the subordinate has come to his own conclusion that the principles are sound. Theory, thus, should aid judgment but not tell one what to do.

Certainly not all agree. Some military leaders believe that leadership can in fact be calculated according to an alluring formula. Antoine-Henri Jomini (1779-1869 CE), a French general serving under the celebrated war hero Napoleon Bonaparte and perhaps the most significant writer of the Napoleonic Wars of the early nineteenth century, viewed leadership as a science, not an art, and would have disagreed with the statement that leadership in combat comprises "infinitely varied circumstances." Jomini perceived warfare in heroic terms and believed that Napoleon's successes could directly be attributed to his adherence to a select number of scientifically determined principles, and his failures to a neglect of adherence to the same.

According to Jomini, military action consists of weapons and techniques as well as political and moral factors. Tactics are determined by the kinds of weaponry used. But only strategy, because of its unchanging nature, can undergo scientific analysis. He thus attempted to prescribe how to make strategic choices intended to "reduce the problem of war to the professional concerns of the wartime commander."[90] He preferred the type of warfare that relied on a mutual agreement between enemies to do battle (in other words, the predictable type), and not the type that relied on the general population murdering "isolated soldiers,"[91] as he described it. This preference might account for his attempts to reduce warfare and leadership to a precise science. Take a moment and ponder the following statement:

> The question has often been discussed, whether it is preferable to assign to the command a general of long experience in service with troops, or an officer of the staff, having generally but little experience in the management of troops. It is beyond question that war is a distinct science of itself, and that it is quite possible to be able to combine operations skillfully without ever having led a regiment against an enemy. Peter the Great, Condé, Frederick, and Napoleon are instances of it. It cannot, then, be denied that an officer from the staff may as well as any other prove to be a great general, but it will not be because he has grown gray in the duties of a quartermaster that he will be capable of the supreme command, but because he has a natural

genius for war and possesses the requisite characteristics.[92]

Jomini suggested that since war is a "distinct science," success does not rely so much on direct experience as on the ability to use theoretical knowledge and calculations. Thus an officer from the staff who has never led a regiment against an enemy may prove to be a great general, particularly if he has a "natural genius," an inborn talent, for war. (Again, are leaders born or made?) Jomini further believed that the scientific approach to war would allow one to create a checklist for action, which could be marked off successfully without considering such factors as human nature, chance, and other uncertainties that might develop during the course of a campaign. He also tended to overlook the possibility of failure. Not only did he select the specific campaigns that best suited his purpose, he failed to follow sound scientific doctrine. In other words, he failed to test the "historical cases in which actual military experience did not conform to prediction based on his principles."[93] While he focused only on the military commanders and their interests—his close proximity to Napoleon and Marshal Ney probably influenced his ambitions—he was vague about "where the principles of war do and do not apply."[94] Sometimes victory depended on adherence to the principles; other times on the military commander.

What we can learn from this is that when the outcome of an act conforms to predictions, it is easy to fall into the trap of believing that the principle used to achieve success will hold true in all situations. However, the analytically driven leader will examine also those cases where the particular principle failed to achieve success. A comparison can be drawn to many modern leadership studies, which likewise tend to rely on the list-type approach, or cookbook for success, as I like to call it. A few examples include: *The 21 Irrefutable Laws of Leadership* by John C. Maxwell and Stephen R. Covey; *The One Minute Manger* by Kenneth H. Blanchard and Spencer Johnson; *Monday Morning Leadership: Eight Mentoring Sessions You Cannot Afford to Miss* by David Cottrell; *The Five Dysfunctions of a Team* by Patrick Lencioni; *The Leadership Moment: Nine Stories of Triumph and Disaster and Their Lessons for Us All* by Michael Useem and Warren Bennis; and *Quiet Leadership: Six Steps to Transforming Performance at Work* by David Rock. Note how each of the aforementioned studies relies on a checklist (Eight Mentoring Sessions, Nine Stories, Six Steps, etc.) that one can memorize and that implies that, if followed, success is more or less guaranteed.

In their book, *The Five Practices of Exemplary Leadership*, authors Jim Kouzes and Barry Posner identify five practices that, if followed, are intended to help leaders get their team to perform extraordinary things. The five practices are: Challenging the Process; Inspiring a Shared Vision; Enabling Others to Act; Modeling the Way; and Encouraging the Heart. It is difficult to criticize the effect that these principles correctly executed would have on the team. Yet their general nature is precisely the reason why it is difficult to disagree, and also why it is difficult to disagree with famous military strategists such as Sun-tzu who have a tendency to state the obvious. The difficulty, of course, lies not in stating the obvious but in bringing the obvious to action.

So who was correct: Carl von Clausewitz in his assertion that, "[e]xperience is of more value in the Art of War than all philosophical truth,"[95] or Jomini in his belief that it is "possible to be able to combine operations skillfully without ever having led a regiment against an enemy"? Regardless of which stand you take, a danger with the checklist approach (or cookbook for success), and with reducing a profoundly human activity such as war and/or leadership to a science, is that it provides a means for avoiding critical thinking.

WHAT ABOUT THE GREAT MEN?

Military history—written by generals, military theorists, historians, revolutionaries, and emperors and kings—has been explored, picked apart, hammered out, examined, categorized, and put back together again. Political and military analysts, proponents and opponents of different theories of war, have used history in attempts to improve battlefield tactics and strategy; to inspire generals and foot soldiers standing at the threshold of armed conflict; and to justify society's position, its "righteousness" to clash with the enemy. The sources we study influence how history is written, but how history is written also influences the availability of the sources. After examining what is on the shelves in bookstores, can we not say the same about leadership studies?

What is the structure of the discipline? We probably agree that leadership is a series of events that were experienced at some point by the author, and that the author believes he or she has an important message to pass on to future generations; in other words, wisdom that future leaders can use according to their own needs, times, and circumstances. No doubt do political and cultural beliefs, as well as personal desires and biases—in short, the needs of the writers and the needs of the users of leadership books—influence the literature of the discipline. Objective interpretation of events is therefore difficult to achieve, and one person's views or experiences may not give us enough practical insight to properly instruct or inspire others. Just as the historian understands that the expressions and intents of the narratives rest with the creators of the works, so must the scholar of leadership understand the importance of examining the sources of the written works. From what point of view do the writers write? What are their educations and backgrounds? What cultural beliefs influence their ideas? Do they draw their knowledge from other sources or are they eyewitnesses to the events they describe? Perhaps most importantly: What are their motivations for writing a particular narrative, and for whom do they write?

Those who are fond of Leading with War and using historical sources of Great Men who, through their character, insight, or compassion have managed to inspire generations of business executives, civilian leaders, and armchair warriors would be wise to remember that historical ideas of the past are seldom timeless, because they can seldom be duplicated and transported to another era flawlessly. The popular view of history at the time the narrative is written is therefore an important issue for consideration, especially if we intend to use the account for instructional purposes at a later date.

Furthermore, our biases and tendency to turn a blind eye to that which we find disagreeable become evident if we do but the briefest examination of the Great Men who have made an impact on history. Sun-tzu in the East and Napoleon Bonaparte in the West are two of the most influential strategic thinkers, despite the fact that Napoleon failed to write detailed accounts of his own campaigns. In America, Civil War general Robert E. Lee undoubtedly takes the lead. By contrast, Adolf Hitler, who theorized about a perfect world, is so despised (justly so, since he was a mass murderer) that we tend to take the greatest care to avoid everything he said, no matter how insightful it might have been. Why? Because war history is often political in nature, and the proponents of a particular view influence the degree to which this view is spread and cross-utilized in other disciplines such as leadership. But surely even Adolf Hitler, Karl Marx, and Mao Zedong had a valuable insight or two to share with us current and future generation leaders? Would you not nod in agreement at the following statements, at least until you learn who said what?

1. We think too small, like the frog at the bottom of the well. He thinks the sky is only as big as the top of the well. If he surfaced, he would have an entirely different view.

2. Reason has always existed, but not always in a reasonable form.

3. Words build bridges into unexplored regions.

Statement number 1 above is attributed to Mao Zedong; number 2 to Karl Marx; and number 3 to Adolf Hitler. I fully expect to take heat or stir controversy with my suggestion that we should acknowledge the insights of our enemies or opposition, even those who we despise the most. But bear in mind that the point of this exercise is not to justify any particular political view or human atrocity, but to demonstrate how we form biases based on the political and cultural influences in our lives. Good leaders need broad horizons, which is all the more reason to develop critical thinking skills, discuss unpleasant facts, and avoid falling in lockstep with the many popular slogans that are so frequently recited in books and at leadership seminars. Although motivational writers and speakers frequently display good advice, it can be misleading if taken out of context or placed in the wrong time or circumstance. When we Lead with War and promote the leadership principles of the great historical generals, we also fall into the trap of using historical examples to justify a belief or viewpoint, or what we perceive to be true as seen from our particular position.

There are, of course, inherent difficulties associated with determining the validity and, therefore, the usefulness of a particular viewpoint. In war, is the foot soldier more correct in his views than the commanding officer, or than the TV viewers for that matter, who experience the war from the safety of their living rooms? In civilian leadership, is the employee more correct in his views than the supervisor or manager, or the customers for that matter, who have an entirely different set of concerns? Or is the commanding officer or the supervisor the higher authority?

In addition to written accounts of war, popular history also includes expressions that grow out of military conflict, for example, *Blitzkrieg*. In contemporary times, expressions such as shock and awe, winning hearts and minds, mother of all wars, and smoke them out of their holes, come to mind. Popular expressions in civilian leadership include, always room for improvement, half-full is better than half-empty, abandon four-letter words, and there is no

"I" in team. These slogans are full of limitations because the needs of the writers and the needs of the users of leadership books (the leaders as well as the followers) differ, and the viewpoints and expressions are essentially as numerous as the writers.

Those who desire to Lead with War and choose to study the Great Men of history should be wary of the fact that Great Men can be categorized into different groups depending on their primary objectives. The first category includes those who write for the purpose of developing war strategy to teach and motivate the recruits in the military academies who read the works. These writers might make inferences between ancient accounts of battles and future war strategies. The second category includes those who are (or were) mere observers of war, for example, the *skalds* (court poets) who accompanied the Norse kings on campaign specifically with the intent of recording what happened and relating it later, usually in verse. The skald had a tough job: Although it was his duty to praise the king, he would lose credibility if he spoke any untruths. Thus if the king were defeated in battle, the skald was left with the difficult task of speaking the truth while still honoring the king with praise of heroism. The third category includes those who have distinguished themselves on campaign and write for the purpose of recording their own greatness, as might be the case, for example, with Julius Caesar, whose "military genius" has been studied and quoted widely. But one wonders, too, what Caesar's motives were when writing the *Commentaries*. Since he was a gifted speaker and writer who employed a sophisticated rhetoric, it is possible that he wrote foremost because he enjoyed listening to his own discourse. The fourth category includes the foot soldiers, or those who have experienced the war firsthand from the most disadvantaged positions. Again, the needs of the writers and the needs of the users of history differ. If leadership books were written primarily by the "foot soldiers" or the employees of civilian corporations, who are subjected to all kinds of leadership principles, would such books as *Who Moved My Cheese?* by Spencer Johnson and Kenneth Blanchard really reach the bestseller list?

Our search for knowledge, whether for instructional or inspirational purposes, binds us at least to an extent to the goals, desires, and individual interpretations of the historians. Whether we study warfare for military purposes or for the education of civilians, the stories of particular wars and Great Men are certainly welcome because they help us identify with our past, search for logical links between past and present or future, and drive home points. But they are not necessarily indicative of how we ought to proceed within our own organization which is often thousands of miles and centuries removed from the event in question.

THE OBVIOUS AND THE NOT SO

While it is tempting to draw parallels between the past and the present, the reasoning we use is not always accurate. The successes and failures of Great Men such as Sun-tzu, Napoleon, and Robert E. Lee can be attributed at least in part to the particular circumstances of their day. Robert E. Lee, for example, faced the daunting task of defending an extensive territory without adequate means, and struggled with the question of whether to invade the North or stay in the South and defend against Union assaults. He reasoned that an offensive-defensive strategy would allow the Confederacy to take the initiative and, after having determined the critical points, muster the forces to attack these points successfully despite the South's inferior strength. He enlisted the help of Stonewall Jackson (1824-1863 CE), who had a reputation for exploiting the enemy by using superior intelligence measures when outnumbered. However, due to his limited manpower resources, Lee's offensive strategy proved questionable at best.

The Confederacy's system of coastal defense also proved inefficient, because the advent of modern guns and the steam engine gave ships greater maneuverability than in the past; an asset that the enemy could use to their advantage when protecting themselves against fire. A combination of Union blockades, amphibious coastal assaults, control of the Mississippi, and almost uninterrupted tries to capture the southern capital further deprived the Confederacy of much needed supplies and weakened Lee's army.[96]

The Confederacy erred because it attempted to wage warfare by using old battlefield concepts in combination with new innovations in weaponry. Although Lee displayed good leadership qualities, relied on cunning advisers, and was truly beloved by his men, the firing technology of the time proved superior to these factors and wiped out large parts of his army. The war naturally took a turn toward attrition and the eventual defeat of the Confederacy.

Sun-tzu faced a different problem. While he had a ready answer to every situation the battlefield commander might encounter, much of China's military history revolves around internal conflicts. Sun-tzu's *Art of War* thus assumes a Chinese opponent and pays little attention to the problems associated with the steppe people and other mounted warriors. It pays even less attention to the skills that a civilian man or woman born into the Western world two and a half millennia later might need to master leadership problems that occur within his or her particular office or organization.

So why do we continue to promote Sun-tzu's *Art of War* as a leadership book for the modern businessman and woman? One reason is because leaders tend to see what they wish to see, and are more accepting of evidence that supports their particular viewpoint than of evidence that challenges it. We tend to find connections between events because we have on our minds those things that we are searching for, while overlooking others. The Chinese texts prove popular because they allow for a broad array of interpretations and can easily be cherry-picked by Western businessmen as they see fit. Saying, "yes, that is true," or "yes, of course, that makes sense," reinforces beliefs that we may already hold, simultaneously allowing us to turn a blind eye to that which is unpleasant.

But any military or civilian leadership model requires an intellectual pursuit that exceeds this "cookbook for success" approach. Those who plaster their walls with isolated sayings and slogans, which are often displayed out of context from the situations in which they first occurred, will not realize true success beyond a temporary "feel good" moment. Although Great Men who have performed admirably in warfare sort of give us a free license to use their stories of heroic struggles as motivation for current and future leaders, we also have a great capacity to misuse much of what history has supposedly taught us. Yes, the leader's job in the workplace is to get the workers to accomplish certain tasks, generally with speed and efficiency. But as one of my professors in military history school taught me, although a checklist may be a good servant, it is not necessarily a good master.[97]

So if not through the checklist, how do you move people to action? Popular passion is necessary, of course, particularly when personal sacrifice is needed. Ancient Greece which is credited with giving birth to democracy or the "rule of many," as defined by Aristotle (384-322 BCE), was hostile to ancient Rome, so naturally many battles were fought. All male citizens were expected to participate in warfare. But in contrast to fighting for the ambitions of a king or dictator, they had a stake in the outcome; they fought for personal freedom and the security of their family, farm, and civilian lifestyle. Defending these ideals paid off on personal terms. If there is no payoff, the leader (or king or dictator or boss) is merely engaging in self-serving interests and cannot expect the team to follow willingly. Sometimes the leader's job is to create popular passion and motivate the team to accept a change that in the leader's mind will lead to greater results; or as is so often stated, to work smarter but not harder. But why should the team want to work smarter? What is the payoff?

In my youth I delivered mail for the post office. It was the best job I have ever had. Each letter carrier was responsible for sorting and delivering the mail to the recipients who lived within his or her district. Whether you worked fast or slow, you still received the same pay for delivering the day's mail to your district. Thus if you could finish the job in three rather than eight hours by working smarter, as frequently happened, you could take the rest of the day off with full pay. It was a win-win for everybody. The customers were happy because they received their mail in the morning instead of the afternoon; the postal workers were happy because they could go home several hours early each day and still get paid as if they had worked eight hours; and the boss was happy because of the many letters and phone calls of praise he received from the customers for the good service. On the other hand, had he reduced the workforce and awarded fewer breaks as "thanks" for the effort, the workers would inevitably have been less eager to work "smarter."

"Progress is made by lazy men looking for easier ways to do things," suggests science fiction writer Robert Heinlein (1907-1988 CE).[98] If you reward the team for working smarter with longer breaks, or perhaps even allow them to go home early with full pay, they will inevitably find a way to work smarter. The ancient Chinese military classic, *T'ai Kung's Six Secret Teachings*, states that in general, "in employing rewards one values credibility; in employing punishments one values certainty. When rewards are trusted and punishments inevitable wherever the eye sees and the ear hears, then even where they do not see or hear there is no one who will not be transformed in their secrecy."[99] The ancient Greek historian and soldier Xenophon likewise reminded us that, "[t]he sweetest of all sounds is praise," and, "[m]en who think that their officer recognizes them are keener to be seen doing something honorable and more desirous of avoiding disgrace."[100] But keep in mind that while rewarding good behavior is honorable, doing nothing when punishment is called for is as bad as being too lenient or too harsh, because by doing nothing, you are in effect failing to reinforce good behavior while giving quiet approval of bad behavior. By failing to punish bad behavior, you are in effect punishing the good workers for their good behavior. If this is the case, then why would any worker want to work smarter? This is so obvious it should go without saying. However, if left unstated, it can with time be forgotten.

What is not obvious? Although you have probably told your team at some point that if it ain't broke there is still room for improvement and half-full is better than half-empty, it is not obvious that it is really so. It is also not obvious that others think like you and like what you think; that there is no "I" in team and together everybody achieves more; or, as Napoleon would have us believe, that secondary matters will settle themselves. If Leading with War is your preferred leadership style, you might want to take to heart the observations of American journalist Robert D. Kaplan: Although "[t]he Army Reserve is desperate for officers . . . there is little urge among American elites to volunteer."[101] What this statement implies is that our leaders are not very eager to sacrifice for their team and cause, even as they are mouthing off about honor and heroism and service to God and country. What do you owe your team, and what does your team owe you outside of what is stated in your written contract? Or do you owe each other nothing but eight hours of work and a paycheck?

HISTORY DOES NOT REPEAT ITSELF

Whether you are a true military man or woman or an armchair warrior who spends your weekends dreaming about leading a group of motivated and talented individuals into battle and emerging a celebrated hero, as evidenced by the difficulty associated with defining it in a single sentence, leadership is not the proprietary domain of a select group of people. One thing that should be learned from war history, or any history for that matter, is that contrary to popular belief history does NOT repeat itself.

History consists of a long row of less than pleasant events. But what sets humans apart from animals is our ability to learn from the accumulated knowledge of those who went before us. Yet when you have worked for a company for twenty years, you have no doubt been through the same cycle of mistakes several times under different leadership, or even more frightening, under the same leadership. As has been said, "Throw a man in the river, and as soon as his clothes have dried, he shall be the same as before." So if history does not repeat itself, then why the same cycle of mistakes? Why do we not learn from the past? As expressed quite eloquently by the ancient Greek philosopher Heraclitus (c. 535-475 BCE), one reason why is because, "[n]o man ever steps in the same river twice, for it is not the same river and he is not the same man."[102]

Historical "cultures" are rarely interchangeable. Take the following example: In 2003 Delta Air Lines created a wholly owned subsidiary called Song Airlines and based it on Southwest Airlines' leadership model: No frills, no first class, no free meals, and quick turnaround time of flights. Song Airlines became an "invitation for a lifestyle."[103] The company advertised for "talent leaders" instead of "team leaders." Song Airlines folded after barely three years of service. Why? Because, contrary to popular belief, history does NOT repeat itself, and when the borrower of an idea fails to heed its own company's history, the adopted "culture" is likely to fail.

We tend to reason by false analogy and draw information from familiar situations of the past in an attempt to relate these to unfamiliar situations of today. But this works only if the past and the present are truly the same and not just appearing similar. Thus while it is tempting to use historical examples as guidelines for future strategy, we should remember that history, as it happens, lacks the benefit of hindsight, and whether a choice is wise or not must often be determined at a later date. We can always look back and say that a particular principle was sound, but we cannot look forward with the same confidence. If Song Airlines had succeeded, we would look back and say that Delta Air Lines made a wise choice. But since we have to rely on hindsight whenever we make a decision for change, and Song Airlines had no history when it was created, we cannot say in advance whether or not our choice will be wise. History might be able to tell us what not to do, but it can rarely tell us what to do. This is one reason why it is difficult to use books such as Sun-tzu's *Art of War* as prescriptions for future strategy. Or as military strategist Carl von Clausewitz reminded us, "[S]kill already developed may be refined by the study of past examples, but skill is only acquired in actually dealing with present examples."[104]

Clausewitz's insights were profound. Although he concluded that historical examples could be used in four ways: to "explain an idea; to demonstrate the application of an idea; to support a statement and so show that a phenomenon was possible; and to give a detailed account of a historical event in order to deduce a doctrine,"[105] he did not suggest that another person's story had universal utility or could be used as an unbiased source that would ultimately lead to success:

> Although using history as a critic and theorist rather than as a historian, Clausewitz was sufficiently historically minded to be aware of the difficulties which sources pose for historians. Equipped with hindsight, they could see things much more clearly than could the commander on the ground, and those who were not practitioners fell back on empty phrases which sounded expert but conveyed little. Reading a general's memoirs was not likely to be much more helpful, because they tended to be selective and self-serving.[106]

Writers of leadership books frequently try to import the concept but not the culture. But if the concept springs from the culture, to truly have a full importation of the concept, the culture must be imported too. Thus if you borrow the military leadership theories of say the Rogue Warrior Richard Marcinko, you must also borrow the rest of the culture upon which his theories are founded. For instance, the Rogue Warrior suggests as one of his Ten Commandments of SpecWar (Special Warfare or Special Operations Forces) that with respect to the team you treat "all alike—just like shit."[107] Would this work within your organization? What do you say, should you treat everyone the same or differently? Should you treat everyone poorly (like shit) until they have proven themselves to you? People are individuals and, although the employees who work under you may be a team, it is their individualism that gives the team its strength. Moreover, individuals react differently to the same treatment. While rough treatment may help some, it will destroy others. How about this: "If you are not tough enough to take a little criticism, you should not be in this position," or, "What does not kill you makes you stronger." Good or bad?

If there is still confusion as to why history appears to repeat itself, consider for a moment the insights of Renaissance Italian political philosopher and Florentine statesman Niccolo Machiavelli: "[W]ise men say, and not without reason, that whoever wishes to foresee the future must consult the past; for human events ever resemble those of preceding times."[108] However, as Machiavelli further explains, the reason why this is so is because men and women of our time are motivated by the same passions as men and women of the past. We therefore let passion rule over reason and frequently repeat mistakes that seem frighteningly similar to those made by generations long gone. This is not the same as saying that we can use examples from the past to build detailed strategies for future success. Moreover, the job of the historian is not merely to state the facts or describe what happened (anybody can do that; it requires only rote memorization), but to bring new views to old events. In concept, this idea can be related to writing poetry or music lyrics. In how many ways can you talk about love or pain, for example? While the old cliché, "there is nothing new under the sun," has continuity, what one acquires is often a result of what one is searching for. New combinations of the old can give the appearance of originality even though there is nothing original about them.

Since the study of history involves not only the study of the facts but also the study of the underlying currents that shaped the events, it is always problematic to transfer one's unique interpretation of what happened in the past to current times or to a different craft. Thus the leadership theories of the Rogue Warrior or any other great general apply to the particular military situation they were developed for and not to all situations and times. Although we may learn from the past, we cannot live in it.[109] Examples from the past can sometimes become what we choose to make of them, but they do not truly foreshadow some future event or even make a point. "The British historian A. J. P. Taylor [1906-1990 CE] once said that the only lesson of history is that there are no lessons. Taylor may be right. Looking for past patterns and precedents and applying them to our own time and circumstances is always risky."[110]

NOTES

[1]Marcus Buckingham and Curt Coffman, *First, Break All the Rules: What the World's Greatest Managers Do Differently* (New York, NY: Simon & Schuster, 1999), 53.

[2]Robert D. Kaplan, "On Forgetting the Obvious," *The American Interest Online* (Jul.-Aug. 2007), http://www.the-american-interest.com/article.cfm?piece=289.

[3]See Ralph Sawyer and Mei-chün Sawyer, *The Seven Military Classics of Ancient China* including the *Art of War* (Boulder, CO: Westview Press, 1993), 139.

[4]See General Tao Hanzhang, *Sun Tzu's Art of War: The Modern Chinese Interpretation*, translated by Yuan Shibing (New York, NY: Sterling Innovation, 2007), 69.

[5]Jeffrey Cohn, "Why We Pick Bad Leaders, and How to Spot the Good Ones," *Special to CNN* (Feb. 14, 2012), http://www.cnn.com/2012/02/14/opinion/cohn-pick-leaders/index.html?hpt=hp_c3.

[6]Jacob Burckhardt, *Quotations on History*, compiled by Robert Blackey, http://history.csusb.edu/facultyStaff/History306/HistoryQuotations8_16_96.pdf.

[7]Jay Luvaas, "Military History: Is It Still Practicable?" *Parameters* (Mar. 1982).

[8]See Sawyer, 162.

[9]Ibid., 161.

[10]Richard Marcinko, *Leadership Secrets of the Rogue Warrior: A Commando's Guide to Success* (New York, NY: Pocket Books, 1996), 129.

[11]Ibid., 155.

[12]See Zhuge Liang, *The Way of the General*, translated by Thomas Cleary, http://kongming.net/novel/writings/wotg/2.php.

[13]See Jennifer Robison, "Lt. General Russel L. Honoré: A Military General's Leadership Lessons," *Gallup Management Journal* (Jan. 8, 2009).

[14]Ibid.

[15]Ibid.

[16]See Owen Connelly, *On War and Leadership: The Words of Combat Commanders from Frederick the Great to Norman Schwarzkopf* (Princeton, NJ: Princeton University Press, 2002), 12.

[17]Ibid.

[18]Donald T. Phillips, *Lincoln on Leadership: Executive Strategies for Tough Times* (New York, NY: Warner Books, 1992), 13.

[19]See H. W. Crocker III, *Robert E. Lee on Leadership: Executive Lessons in Character, Courage, and Vision* (New York, NY: Three Rivers Press, 2004), Kindle Edition.

[20]See Marcinko, *Leadership Secrets of the Rogue Warrior*, 72.

[21]Ibid., 108.

[22]See Richard Marcinko, *The Rogue Warrior's Strategy for Success: A Commando's Principles of Winning* (New York, NY: Pocket Books, 1997), 13.

[23]Ibid., 94.

[24]Chuck Yeager, Famous Quotes, http://www.icelebz.com/quotes/chuck_yeager/.

[25]Richard Hiner, "Instructor Report," *Air Safety Foundation* (First Quarter, 2005).

[26]Snorri Sturluson, *King Olaf Trygvason's Saga*, Internet Sacret Text Archive, http://www.sacred-texts.com/neu/heim/07olaftr.htm.

[27]See Nassir Ghaemi, *A First-Rate Madness: Uncovering the Links Between Leadership and Mental Illness* (New York, NY: Penguin Press, 2011), Kindle Edition.

[28]See Marcinko, *Leadership Secrets of the Rogue Warrior,* 6.

[29]Ghaemi.

[30]Thucydides, *The Peloponnesian War: The Complete Hobbes Translation* with notes and introduction by David Grene (Chicago, IL: University of Chicago Press, 1989), 1-2.

[31]Ibid., 3.

[32]Ibid., 32.

[33]Ibid., 50.

[34]Ibid., 67.

[35]Ibid., 46.

[36]Ibid., 67-68.

[37]See Thucydides, *The History of the Peloponnesian War*, Kindle Edition.

[38]Ibid.

[39]Xenophon, *The March Up Country: A Translation of Xenophon's Anabasis*, translated by W. H. D. Rouse (Ann Arbor: MI: University of Michigan Press, 2001), 91.

[40]Ibid., 99.

[41]Ibid., 96-97.

[42]Ibid., 95.

[43]Ibid., 98.

[44]Ibid., 90.

[45]Ibid., 89.
[46]Ibid., 109.
[47]See Julius Caius Caesar, *De Bello Gallico & Other Commentaries of Caius Julius Caesar*, translated by W. A. Macdevitt (1929), 9.
[48]Ibid., 4.
[49]Ibid., 5.
[50]Ibid., 2.
[51]Ibid., 2.
[52]Ibid., 6.
[53]Ibid., 12.
[54]Ibid., 26.
[55]Ibid., 6.
[56]Ibid., 20.
[57]Ibid., 3.
[58]Ibid., 15.
[59]Ibid., 15.
[60]Johann von Ewald, *Diary of the American War: A Hessian Journal*, translated and edited by Joseph P. Tustin (New Haven, CT: Yale University Press, 1979), 21.
[61]Ibid., 18.
[62]Ibid., 25.
[63]Ibid., 19.
[64]Ibid., 42.
[65]Ibid., 42.
[66]Ibid., 45.
[67]Ibid., 354.
[68]Ibid., 44.
[69]Ibid., 355.
[70]Ibid., 354.
[71]Ibid., 355.
[72]Ibid., 356.
[73]Ibid., 361.

[74]Ibid., 34.

[75]See Armand de Caulaincourt, *With Napoleon in Russia: The Memoirs of General de Caulaincourt, Duke of Vicenza* (New York, NY: William Morrow, 1935), 48.

[76]Ibid., 63.

[77]Ibid., 87.

[78]Ibid., 103.

[79]Ibid., 52.

[80]Ibid., 60.

[81]Ibid., 61.

[82]Ibid., 46.

[83]Ibid., 49.

[84]Ibid., 64.

[85]Ibid., 67.

[86]Ibid., 70.

[87]Ibid., 72.

[88]See Russell F. Weigley, *The American Way of War: A History of United States Military Strategy and Policy* (Bloomington, IN: Indiana University Press, 1973), 215.

[89]See Carl von Clausewitz, *On War*, edited and translated by Michael Howard and Peter Paret (Princeton, NJ: Princeton University Press, 1976), 193.

[90]See John Shy, *Makers of Modern Strategy: From Machiavelli to the Nuclear Age*, edited by Peter Paret (Princeton, NJ: Princeton University Press, 1986), 167.

[91]Antoine-Henri Jomini, *The Art of War*, translated by H. Mendell and W. P. Craighill (Philadelphia, PA: Lippincott, 1879), Article VIII.

[92]Ibid., Article XIV.

[93]Shy, 173.

[94]Ibid., 174.

[95]Carl von Clausewitz, *On War: A Modern Military Classic* (Radford, VA: Wilder Publications, 2008), 133.

[96]See Allan R. Millett and Peter Maslowski, *For the Common Defense: A Military History of the United States of America* (New York, NY: The Free Press, 1994), 172-173.

[97]From H. P. Willmott lecture about *Jomini and The Art of War*, Norwich University, VT, 2006.

[98]See Ian Morris, *Why the West Rules—For Now* (New York, NY: Farrar, Straus and Giroux, 2010), 27.

[99]See Sawyer, 51.

[100]See Quotes Papa, *16 Xenophon Quotes and Sayings*, http://www.quotespapa.com/authors/xenophon-quotes.html.

[101]Kaplan.

[102]Heraclitus, Wikiquote, http://en.wikiquote.org/wiki/Heraclitus.

[103]See PBS, "The Persuaders," *Frontline*, http://www.pbs.org/wgbh/pages/frontline/shows/persuaders/view/.

[104]See Dallas D. Irvine, "The French Discovery of Clausewitz and Napoleon," *The Journal of the American Military Institute*, Vol. 4, No. 3 (Autumn 1940), 144.

[105]See Hew Strachan, *Clausewitz's On War* (New York, NY: Atlantic Monthly Press, 2007), 97.

[106]Ibid., 98-99.

[107]See Marcinko, *Leadership Secrets of the Rogue Warrior*, frontmatter.

[108]Niccolo Machiavelli, *The Historical, Political, and Diplomatic Writings of Niccolo Machiavelli*, Vol. 2, translated by Christian E. Detmold (Boston, MA: James R. Osgood and Company, 1882), 422.

[109]See Michael C. C. Adams, *The Best War Ever: America and World War II* (Baltimore, MD: The John Hopkins University Press, 1994), 5.

[110]Aaron David Miller, *The Much Too Promised Land: America's Elusive Search for Arab-Israeli Peace* (New York, NY: Bantam Dell, 2008), 127.

About the Author

Martina Sprague has a Master of Arts Degree in Military History from Norwich University in Vermont. As a historian she is particularly interested in political and social factors that influence the decisions of "Great Men" and the actions of their subordinates. She has written numerous books about military and political/social history. For more information, please visit her Web site: www.modernfighter.com.

www.ingramcontent.com/pod-product-compliance
Lightning Source LLC
Chambersburg PA
CBHW071620170526
45166CB00003B/1128